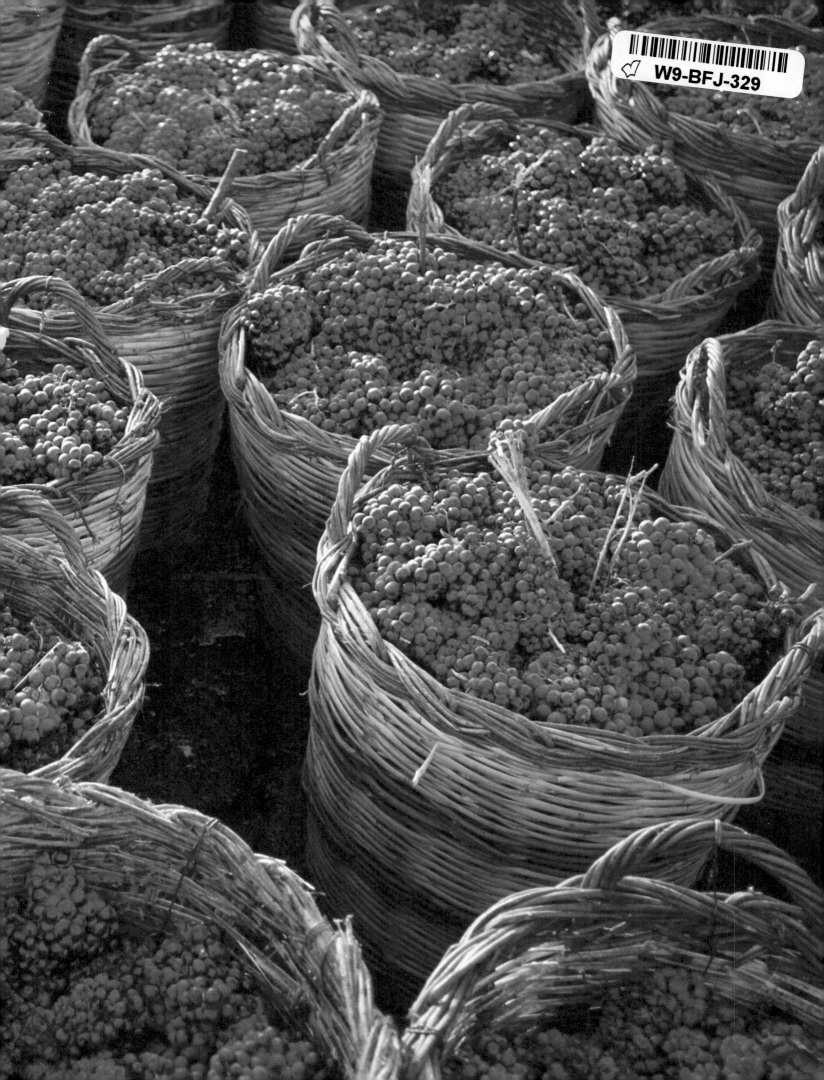

Greece
and the Greek Islands

This book was devised and produced by
Multimedia Publications (UK) Ltd

Editor: Marilyn Inglis
Production: Julia Mather
Design: John Strange
Picture Research: Tessa Paul

First published in the United States of
America 1985 by Gallery Books, an imprint of
W. H. Smith Publishers Inc., 112 Madison
Avenue, New York, NY 10016

ISBN 0 8317 3936 3

Typeset by Flowery
Origination by C. L. G.
Printed in Italy by Sagdos

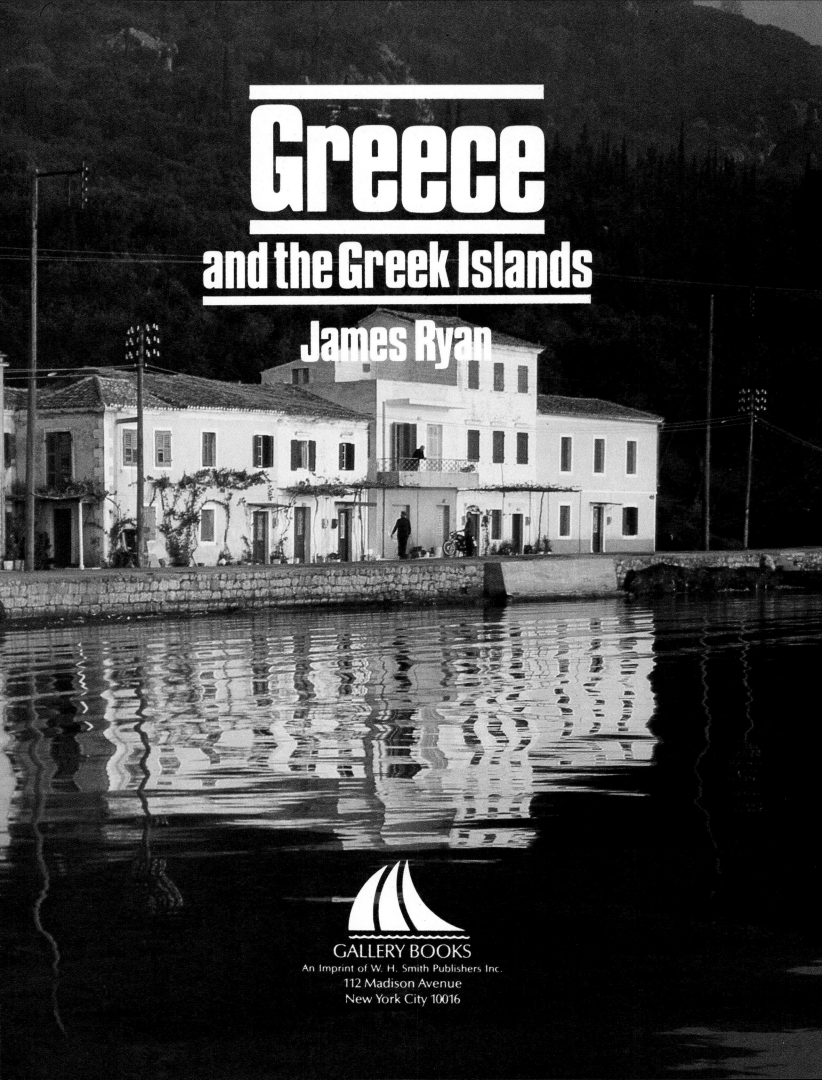

Greece
and the Greek Islands

James Ryan

GALLERY BOOKS
An Imprint of W. H. Smith Publishers Inc.
112 Madison Avenue
New York City 10016

The Theater of Dionysus in Athens once held
15,000 spectators for performances of plays
by Euripides, Aeschylus and others. This frieze
dates from the fourth century BC.

Half title page
Nets drying, Astypalia.

Title page
Corfu waterfront.

CONTENTS

The port of Piraeus is the gateway to Athens.
In the harbor small fishing vessels share
seaway with intercontinental liners.

The Mother of Civilization

To the foreign visitor with a sense of history, Greece is overwhelming. No other country can claim to have contributed so much to western civilization. Our idea of what is beautiful begins with the gorgeous figures of men, women and gods sculpted in marble two and a half thousand years ago. Architecture seems scarcely to have advanced since Pericles cast eyes upon the Parthenon. To Greece we owe the theater, the Olympic games, much of our language and the very structure of our thought embodied in philosophy. Perhaps most precious of all our inheritance is democracy — a Greek word meaning government by the people.

Indeed, there is much about Greece that has not changed. The power of ancient times was built on mastery of the sea. The ancients used to call the Mediterranean "the road", and it was their central position between Western Europe and the East which provided them with such profitable opportunities for trade. Today Greece possesses the world's largest merchant fleet, as the Onassis family and many others could testify.

But the weight of ancient history sits lightly upon the shoulders of modern Greece. Proud of their inheritance and fiercely conscious of the struggles of recent centuries, the most important moment is emphatically *now*. This sensual enjoyment of the present explains many things which at first puzzle — and even irritate — the visitor from abroad. Step from the airplane, and begin the difficult process of adapting to a different conception of time.

It would be wrong to assume that since you have a ferry connection for 5 p.m. at Piraeus to travel to Aegina there will in fact be transportation there at that hour. That depends on a number of factors... You will almost certainly be too early, but possibly too late. As a rule of thumb, performances at the theater will begin perhaps half an hour behind the advertized schedule. Equally, an appointment with Greek friends will indicate the hour before which one's engagement will *not* begin rather than the time at which it will.

A few days in Greece will take the edge off these apparently unforgivable lapses. It is the sense of the present which gives Greek life the exuberance lacking in more literal societies. Why destroy enjoyment of the present by imposing plans for an uncertain future? What, after all, is wrong with now?

Right: The march of progress has changed little in this scene. Corn and red peppers dry in the sun.

Far right: In a typical scene, men sit in the shade outside a *kafeneion* — coffee house — waiting for the cool of evening to descend. This is Ios, a small island in the Cyclades, said to be the resting place of Homer. He could not have found a more peaceful place. Although now popular with tourists, Ios is still renowned for its spotless beauty: even the mortar between the sidewalk stones is painted white.

Below: On the island of Mykonos, whitewashed houses and tiny chapels tumble in a twisting confusion of narrow streets until they meet the harbor waters. Nothing could be more practical for the street trader than a pair of hand-held scales and a donkey to carry her wares.

Above: A fisherman is untangling his nets, a job which must be done every day after the morning's catch has been landed. This is the island of Milos, where the Venus de Milo was found. (It was taken away to the Louvre in Paris.) On Milos fishermen use as boathouses seaside caves where troglodytes once lived.

Far right: A *caique* anchored at Zakinthos, the southernmost Ionian island. Boats like this one are often used for sightseeing trips.

It is normal to sit for hours at a table outside the local *kafeneion* without facing pressure to drink up and order more. In fact, it is not unknown to walk into a taverna and be offered food free — and any attempt to pass money would be considered offensive. The Greeks must be the most hospitable people on earth.

Do not expect a great deal to happen between 1 and around 3 p.m. (it may be 5 p.m., depending on the situation). Nor is it to be expected that food will be served in the evening before 9 o'clock. This is partly explained by the Mediterranean custom of observing the *siesta* (or *mesimeri* in Greek), but if it were a question simply of avoiding the rigors of the midday sun it would be hard to explain why work stops for several hours after noon during the winter too.

To be honest, the cuisine is not wonderful (though a maritime nation cannot fail to offer delicious seafood). Ironically some of the best "Greek" delicacies have distinctly Turkish association: "moussaka", "baklava"

and "halva" are all Turkish words. Even the thick, sweet coffee which is consumed in great quantities in every roadside *kafeneion* is suspiciously similar to what elsewhere is known as "Turkish" coffee.

The signs of Orthodox Christianity are everywhere. Greece is the most thoroughly religious nation in the West, if proportionate membership of the Church is a yardstick. The influence of the Church is everywhere — in the wayside shrines which decorate the roadsides, in the black-robed priests who preside over every major event in social life. Everyone is named after a saint: in Corfu this practise reaches extraordinary proportions — more than half of the male population is called Spiro after the island's patron saint Spiridon.

Watching an old woman driving her laden mule through winding streets of whitewashed houses, it is easy to believe that time has stood still. But Greece combines past and present with effortless ease. The combination enriches all of us.

Above: A family shrine, Corfu. Monuments of this kind, large and small, are scattered along the waysides of Greece. They are usually dedicated to a particular saint, or they may commemorate an event which took place in the vicinity.

Above: Camomile drying on a windowsill in Crete.

Left: The poet Seferis said of his native Paros that the organization of the streets and squares aspires to the condition of music. The town shimmers with a sparkling array of colors: here a bougainvillea caps a doorway.

Left: Even the monasteries were too easily accessible for some hermits. These cliff-face dwellings can be reached only by rope ladder.

Far left: The Monastery of Ayia Triada (Holy Trinity) perches giddily atop one of the giant columns of Meteora. There are some 30 rocks here, rising sheer from the valley floor to heights of between 600 and 900 feet. The first "monastery in the sky" was founded more than 600 years ago by a monk named Athanasius, who was in search of a place of perfect seclusion. By the sixteenth century there were 24 monasteries, but now only five are inhabited by monks or nuns.

15

Inside the Palace of Knossos, Crete. This was the center of the Minoan civilization, which dominated the Aegean until its sudden destruction around 1400 BC.

CHAPTER 2

Gods and Heroes

Every civilization has its explanation for the beginning of things. For the ancient Greeks, it all started with Chaos. From Chaos emerged Ge, Mother Earth, and she somehow produced a son, Uranus or Heaven. Seeing his mother's nakedness, Uranus wept — and so there appeared seas, rivers and lakes. They stimulated the growth of flowers and animals.

Uranus and Ge produced a series of peculiar offspring: Giants, one-eyed Cyclopses, and then Titans. Led by Cronos (Time), the Titans overthrew their parents and divided the world between them. But Cronos was in turn dethroned by his son Zeus (or Jupiter, as the Romans called him), assisted by brothers Poseidon and Hades. These three drew lots: Zeus won the skies, Poseidon the seas, and Hades had to make do with the underworld. But Zeus was always the strongest, having invented the thunderbolt. He married his sister Hera, and they settled on Mount Olympus.

This may sound complicated, and not a little implausible, but it is only the beginning. In fact the Greeks recognized several hundred gods and goddesses, related to one another in various extraordinary ways. There were also demigods (half god, half human) and spirits such as nymphs and naiads. And then, it was not unknown for humans to achieve the status of demigod or god as over the centuries their virtues achieved ever-greater recognition: Aesculapius, (Aslepius), god of healing, seems to have been elevated in this way.

Collectively the Greek gods are known as the Pantheon. They were seldom *good*, and one was not expected to emulate their often atrocious behavior. But each was a force to be reckoned with, respected and won over to the right side. They represented, perhaps, aspects of the human character or features of the natural

Above: The Parthenon, centerpiece of the Acropolis in Athens. Dedicated to the virgin goddess Athena, patroness of the city, it was built in the fifth century BC on the instructions of Pericles. It was home to the goddess's virgin priestesses, and also housed the city's treasure and bullion. In later times it was used as a church dedicated to the Virgin Mary, and then as a Turkish arsenal. Despite the ravages of time, the honey-colored marble edifice of the Parthenon still soars above the city.

world. As such, they helped explain the inexplicable, but they did not bring order to an uncertain world.

Athena was goddess of wisdom. A daughter of Zeus, she was patroness of the arts and crafts. According to the myth, she was born fully armed from her father's head, and this is why she is often depicted in military attire.

Apollo, son of Zeus, had the job of driving the chariot of the sun across the skies each day. He was lord of archery and sudden death, but also of music.

Artemis, Apollo's twin sister, was goddess of the moon. She was also adept with bow and arrow, and she watched over hunters.

Ares was the god of war and curse of mankind. Hated also by his fellow gods, he

went into battle accompanied by his sons Fear and Panic.

Aphrodite, a cousin of Zeus, was the most beautiful of all the goddesses. Hera was jealous of her and obliged her to marry the lame Hephaestus, god of blacksmiths. Unhappy in her own personal life, she was nevertheless protectress of lovers as well as goddess of gardens.

Hermes was the messenger of the gods. He protected traders and travelers, and was patron of boxing and racing.

Pan resembled a goat. He invented the pan-pipes and watched over shepherds and their flocks.

The ancient Greeks would not have been surprised to meet one of the gods in the street, especially since they were in the habit of disguising themselves as mortals.

Above: This gold medal from Macedonia was struck in the third century for a victor in the Olympic Games.

Left: The Ruins of the Temple of Hera at Olympia, site of the original games. Here, from 776 BC, Greeks would gather every fourth year to compete in athletic and artistic events.

What has surprised modern scholars is that many of the heroes of Greek legend — second only to the gods in status — seem really to have existed.

Theseus was the legendary prince of Athens, founder of the city's greatness. According to the story, the tyrannical King Minos of Crete (probably an amalgam of several historical figures) regularly demanded from Athens a tribute of seven youths and seven maidens to satisfy the appetite of the Minotaur, a monster with a bull's head on a human body, concealed within a labyrinth. Theseus volunteered as one of the victims, and with the assistance of Minos' daughter Ariadne and her famous thread he managed to slay the creature and find his way out again. It is not unreasonable to read into this story a romantic rendering of the decline of Cretan power in favor of Aegean civilization.

Agamemnon, leader of the expedition against Troy, was held to have been King of Mycenae. It was at the end of the nineteenth century that the archeologist Heinrich Schliemann uncovered the ruins of both cities, buried for almost 3000 years. He also discovered a burial mask which some believe belonged to the great king himself.

Accompanying Agamemnon on his expedition was Odysseus, central figure in Homer's *Odyssey,* which is perhaps the greatest story of all time. The existence of Homer as a historical figure was once doubted, but today we have good evidence that Homer was born on the island of Chios in the Aegean. As for Odysseus, he really was king of the Ionian island of Ithaca, just as the story tells. Homer relates that while Odysseus was away at war a host of suitors besieged his wife Penelope with the intention of persuading her that her husband was dead and that she should remarry. She steadfastly refused. Eventually Odysseus returned after a long and mostly unfortunate journey throughout the Aegean. Athena disguised him so that he could take his enemies by surprise, and it was some time before his identity was recognized.

The Venus de Milo, sculpted around 100 BC. Known to the Greeks as Aphrodite, she was the goddess of love.

Above: Alexander the Great astride his horse Bucephalus. According to legend Philip of Macedon, Alexander's father, bought this beautiful black stallion for a huge sum, but neither he nor his best horsemen could tame it. The eight-year-old Alexander, realizing that Bucephalus was being frightened by its own shadow, turned it toward the sun, mounted it and rode off at lightning speed. Alexander took the horse on all his military campaigns, and named a city after it. When it died it was given a state funeral.

Above left: Hermes, sculpted around 325 BC by Praxiteles for the Temple of Hera at Olympia. The infant is Dionysūs; he is probably trying to grasp a bunch of grapes which Hermes is holding in his right hand, now unfortunately missing. Praxiteles perhaps more than any other artist brought life and realism to Greek sculpture.

Left: A gold funeral mask from one of the shaft graves in Mycenae, held by some to be the mask of Agamemnon himself.

The Agora, or ancient market-place, in Athens. This is the Stoa of Attalus, a shopping mall originally built in the second century BC. It was later destroyed, but was beautifully reconstructed by American archeologists in the 1960s.

A view over the rooftops of Athens toward the Acropolis.

Glorious Heritage

"Future ages will wonder at us, as the present age wonders at us now." Those were the words of Pericles, ruler of Athens in the fifth century BC when the city's power was at its height and its cultural life most glorious. Pericles had reason to be proud for he had commissioned the building of the Parthenon, centerpiece of the Acropolis, the great limestone rock where the city began and which boasts her principal shrines. By moonlight or at sunset, or in the crisp air of early morning it is a magnificent and unforgettable sight.

There is only one approach and, as the visitor struggles up the steep slope of the Sacred Way (the highest point of the Acropolis is 200 feet above the city), it is not difficult to remember that the Acropolis was first a city fortress.

There are four surviving monuments on the Acropolis, and the first is the Propylaea, a monumental gateway and one of the masterpieces of Greek architecture. Also commissioned by Pericles, it was in fact never completed, apparently because it threatened to eclipse other sanctuaries nearby. It has suffered a great deal of damage over the centuries, but restoration work has been discreet and a large part of the building is still standing. It has excellent examples of columns in both Ionic and Doric styles (the two main Classical forms).

To the right of the Propylaea is the temple of Athene Nike, also known as Wingless Victory — because the wily Greeks showed Nike (Victory) wingless to prevent her from flying away. The temple was built to commemorate two stunning victories against the Persian Empire which finally forced it to sue for peace. With its delicate columns glistening in the sun, one side of the building faces towards Marathon, site of a land battle in 490 BC. Marathon is 26 miles from Athens, and it was the famous nonstop run of a messenger to report the

The Temple of Athena Nike.

victory which has given us the name of the athletic event. A second side of the temple faces Salamis, where the Greeks again defeated the Persians, this time in a naval battle.

The third building of the Acropolis is the Erechtheion, named after a legendary Athenian king. According to legend, it was on the site of this temple that Athena and Poseidon fought for control of Attica. Athena won the contest after offering the Attic mortals an olive tree — a useful contribution indeed — but the temple's builders dedicated it to both gods all the same, just to play safe. Architecturally the Erechtheion is remarkable for the Caryatids, statues of maidens which acted as columns to support the roof. The statues in place now are copies: the originals were removed to the safety of the Acropolis Museum because they were suffering too

greatly from the pollution created by the modern city (and one Caryatid was spirited away to the British Museum in London by Lord Elgin in 1901). Nevertheless, the elegant and refined Erechtheion remains a magnificent architectural achievement.

Nothing, however, can rival the Parthenon. Built between 447 and 432 BC, it has 17 fluted columns on either side and eight at each end. It is renowned for its light and graceful symmetry, all the more remarkable because there is not a straight line in the building. The architect, Ictinos, had noticed that flat surfaces appear to sag in the middle, and straight columns seem to bulge outward. So he designed every piece of the building to be slightly irregular to overcome the illusion.

In the time of Pericles the Parthenon and its sister buildings would have been brightly painted, as would the statues

Left: Removing the Caryatids from the Acropolis for safe keeping.

Below: The south portico of the Erechtheion, showing replicas in place of the original Caryatids.

within and around them. We are fortunate to see them without the paint, for the marble used is magnificent, changing color according to the seasons and time of day. In other respects time has ill-treated the Parthenon. All around the building ran a frieze depicting participants in the ceremonial Panathenaic Procession, which took place every four years at the festival known as the Great Panathenaea. The frieze showed riders and horses, virgins, priests, and so on, sculpted with a rare combination of vigor and delicacy. Today only a small proportion remains in place. Parts of it may be found in the Acropolis Museum, other sections are in London and Paris, while some were destroyed in an explosion in 1687. At the time the Parthenon was being used by the controlling Turkish army to store gunpowder. A shell fired by their Italian enemies scored a direct hit, and there was great destruction. The roof of the temple was blown off, and much else was lost besides.

Even so, whether seen by day or floodlit by night, the Parthenon remains perhaps the most sublime piece of architecture ever created by mankind.

One of the most glorious experiences offered by modern Athens is the *son et lumière* — a dramatic presentation of the city's history in sound and light. The backcloth to this spectacle, staged after sunset between April and October, is the Acropolis itself. Every evening an expectant and excited audience gathers to watch the spectacle from a nearby hill called the Pnyx which was the seat of the Assembly where Pericles, Themistocles, Demosthenes and other great orators addressed the citizens — some of their speeches can still be read. The English-language performances usually begin at 9.15 p.m.

Just below the Acropolis there are reminders of another great gift to the world from Classical Athens — the theater.

In early times a festival was held every year in honor of Dionysus, god of wine and revelry (he was known to the Romans as Bacchus). He was often depicted as a goat. Along with less seemly celebrations, it became customary for songs to be sung in the god's praise (the word "tragedy" means "goat's song"). These tragedies became more and more sophisticated, until they

A detail of the Parthenon, viewed from the northeast. The marble used in this building, from nearby Mount Pentelicus, is rich in iron ore, giving it a deep brown color in some lights.

Above: The Parthenon was built without the use of mortar. The columns were pieced together with joints so tight that they can hardly be seen even today. The walls were made of blocks held together with cramp-irons and melted lead.

Left: A photographer accompanies the present-day masters of the Acropolis – cats.

Above: Contemporary performance of *Antigone* by Sophocles. This play tells the story of the conflict between a king whose conscience is governed by reasons of state, and a woman for whom compassion is a higher law. First performed 2400 years ago, this tragedy still moves audiences today.

Right: The Temple of Olympian Zeus. The roof was originally supported by 104 huge columns; now only 16 remain.

developed during the Golden Age (480-430 BC) into the art form perfected by Aeschylus, Euripides, Sophocles and others such as Aristophanes who wrote light-hearted plays called "comedies".

Two theaters are to be found below the Acropolis, the Theater of Dionysus and the Odeon of Herodes Atticus. The first was built in the fourth century BC to replace a wooden structure on the same site in which the plays of Sophocles, Euripides, Aeschylus and Aristophanes were first performed. It would have held perhaps 17,000 spectators (despite Plato's estimate of 30,000), and fragments of 25 of the 64 circular tiers of seats remain, together with a number of thrones which were reserved for priests or other dignitaries.

The Odeon, which dates from Roman times, would have seated between 5000 and 6000, and was one of the last great public buildings to be put up in Athens. It has been restored to excellent condition, and ancient and modern plays are staged there every summer, with orchestral, operatic and ballet performances during the Athens Festival (July-September). The setting is matchless, the ocher-colored Roman stonework glowing brilliantly in the floodlighting, which includes, of course, the Acropolis itself.

After the death of Pericles (429 BC), Athens entered a turbulent period—first there was the Peloponnesian War and then the rise of Macedon under Philip and his son Alexander the Great. Later came the Romans, and under their rule Athens lost its military role, settling into a quieter life as the university city of the civilized world.

Artistic and cultural creativity did not pass away with the death of Pericles. Business continued to prosper in the commercial hub of the Agora—an assembly-place where traders rubbed shoulders with administrators and where the philosophers Socrates, Plato and Aristotle used to gather their followers to debate the foundations of knowledge. Later,

The Theater of Herodes Atticus. The seating, stage and *orchestra* (the semicircular or circular area where the action in classical plays mostly took place) have been carefully reconstructed for use today.

St. Paul used to go there daily to dispute and to seek converts to his new faith. It was the center of public life.

The Agora has been excavated, and the foundations of the buildings identified—temples, administrative buildings, shops—but the scene strikes the layman as sprawling confusion, since none of the buildings are standing and it is not always easy to identify the foundations among the rubble and broken slabs of marble. But you can imagine the cheerful, lively bustle, with the crowded markets, the barbers' shops, the moneychangers, the priests, the beggars and the merchants.

Under Roman administration a new marketplace was constructed not far from the old. Here can be found the magnificent Tower of the Winds, an octagon built in marble by the astronomer Androkinos of Kyrrhos in the first century BC. It served the triple purpose of public sundial, water-clock and weather-vane. Its eight sides face the eight winds into which the compass was divided, and the sculpture depicts the figures of the eight winds.

The Emperor Hadrian was very fond of Athens in his typically grandiose way. He planned a new city, to be called Hadrianopolis, and erected a marble arch to mark its beginnings. The façades, otherwise identical, bear the two inscriptions: "This is Athens, the ancient city of Theseus," and "This is the city of Hadrian and not of Theseus." The combination of Greek and Roman styles has a rather ungainly effect.

Hadrian was also responsible for overseeing the completion of the Olympeion, or the Temple of Olympian Zeus, which took 700 years to build—"a great victory of time" Philostratus called it. It was the largest temple in Greece. Hadrian could not resist putting a colossal statue of himself inside it to accompany the statue of the god when he visited the city to dedicate the temple in AD 130.

Right: Front-row seats — reserved for noble patrons of the arts and, in the center opposite the altar of the god, the high priest — in the Theater of Dionysus.

Below: A panoramic view of the same theater, showing clearly how the Greeks took advantage of a natural hollow in the hillside. In Roman times a water conduit was built around the *orchestra* so that mock naval battles could be staged. Wild animal shows were also put on here.

The owners of front-row seats had their names inscribed on them, so there could be no mistake!

A carter makes his way along a jetty at
Piraeus.

CHAPTER 4

Cities and Sights

In the eleventh and twelfth centuries AD Byzantine civilization began to present cultural offerings in Athens fit to stand beside those of earlier ages. The Church of the Holy Apostles near the Agora dates from this period (though the wall-paintings are from the seventeenth century). Some way out of the center of town on the slopes of Mount Hymettus, the eleventh-century Kaiseriani Monastery is an oasis of tranquility. Built at the source of the river Ilissos (now running underground), the monks provided themselves with a mill, bakery, bath-house, refectory and church amid the shade of cypress, pine and plane trees.

A remarkable sight is the little Metropolis, also known as Aghios Eleutherios. Erected in the twelfth century, it is a mere 40 ft by 25 ft and is constructed entirely from ruins of earlier monuments.

But Byzantine art and architecture scarcely had time to mature before the Turks asserted their domination over Athens. The Mosque of Tzistarakis, built in 1759, dates from those days — though now it has been converted into the Museum of Greek Popular Art. It is here and in the Byzantine Museum that the finest examples of embroidery and religious artefacts may be viewed.

MODERN ATHENS
One hundred and fifty years ago, Athens was a Turkish town with 5000 inhabitants. Now, with a population of more than two and a half million, it is a major commercial city.

It cannot be said that the explosion of building which occurred following independence in 1830 (and which continues to this day) has resulted in a beautiful city. Jostling those famous Classical monuments are a mass of apartment blocks, offices, shops and other buildings.

There are landmarks, of course—Syntagma (or Constitution) Square, adorned with fountains and orange trees; equally famous is Omonia Square, daytime focus for the city's sidewalk life where stalls and kiosks offer everything from seeded rolls to shoelaces.

At night it is the Plaka around which life revolves. Steep and narrow streets nestling beneath the walls of the Acropolis are packed to overflowing with tavernas, bars and discos. After the bleaching heat of the afternoon sun, the cooler hours of evening awaken appetites. Or, strictly speaking, it is the *ouzo* and *mezedes* which do that—fierce aniseed drinks accompanied by morsels of cheese, meat or melon. The meal does not begin before eight, and is unlikely to end before midnight. Here traditional Greek music is played and sung and dances danced.

THESSALONIKI

Thessaloniki, often known as Salonica, is the second city of Greece, with a population of more than half a million. A commercial and industrial center, its long history sits very lightly on its shoulders. This is largely because its strategic geographical position has ensured that successive waves of invaders were particularly keen to conquer the city, and wrought much destruction as they did so.

The city was founded by a successor to Alexander the Great who sought to bolster his claims to the succession by marrying Alexander's half-sister Thessaloniki and naming a city in her honor. By the time the aspostle Paul visited, it was an important trading city of the Roman Empire. St. Paul's Epistles to the Thessalonians are among the earliest documents of the Christian Church.

Above: A gold coin minted in the time of Justinian I, who became Emperor of Byzantium in 527. A Christian ruler, he closed the Athenian schools of philosophy and law in 529, but by then they were mere shadows of the days of Socrates and Plato.

Left: The monastery at Kaiseriani, on the slopes of Mount Hymettus, commands magnificent views of Athens stretching across the valley below. The church inside the monastery, founded in the eleventh century, possesses some attractive post-Byzantine frescoes.

Far left: A procession on Tinos. On August 15 every year Orthodox pilgrims from all over the world gather on this small island for the Festival of the Tiniotissa, the Virgin of Tinos, whose icon is said to work miracles.

Far left: Modern Athens, unplanned and anarchic, is a confusion of styles and ways of life. Alongside the high-rise offices and apartment blocks nestle narrow lanes and humble dwellings which would not be out of place in a distant island village.

Left: This street vendor will sell you ice cream and a variety of other snacks.

Below: Luscious apples on a stall – but the priest seems more interested in acquiring a chicken!

From Roman times there survives a triumphal arch erected by the Emperor Galerius in his own honor. More numerous are the remnants of Byzantine times, when Thessaloniki was second only to Byzantium itself in importance. At one time there were 360 churches in the city, it is said; now some 20 remain, and of those nine possess important mosaics and icons. Until recently the city was also noted for its large Jewish population, descendants of refugees from Spain in the fifteenth century. But during the Germany occupation in World War II almost all of the 60,000 Jewish population was deported to Poland, and only one tenth survived.

Today Thessaloniki, while not a beautiful city, vibrates with commercial life. An annual fair provides the focus for trading activity in the northern Aegean. And an increasing number of visitors pass through each year on their way to the newly developed tourist centers of the Halkidiki Peninsula. But travelers in too great a hurry will miss the opportunity to take an evening meal in Panorama, a hillside village aptly named, for it offers magnificent views of the bay and city laid out below.

MOUNT ATHOS
Sited on the easternmost peninsula of Halkidiki is the unique monastic community

of Mount Athos. Here are 20 monasteries, joined together to provide their own form of government. The autonomy of Mount Athos was recognized by the Greek government in the 1920s. Today the area is administered by a council of four members and an assembly of 20, one representative from each monastery. Seventeen of the monasteries are Greek, one Bulgarian, one Serbian and one Russian.

There are numerous other small religious settlements which are subject to one or other of the ruling monasteries. Some of the monks live the lives of hermits in the empty, rugged hills, and the seclusion of the area is protected. It is possible for male visitors to enter some of the monasteries, but women are forbidden to set foot on Mount Athos by an ordinance dating back 1000 years.

DELPHI

Perched 2000 feet up on the slopes of Mount Parnassus, Delphi is halfway to heaven. For the ancients it was an especially sacred place. It was thought to be the center of the earth, and it was the headquarters of the cult of the god Apollo. While war raged across Greece between rival city states, Delphi was declared a trucial zone.

The main event of the year was the festival of Apollo. States vied with each other to present the most lavish gifts to the god: their offerings were stored in the treasuries whose ruins can be seen along the path to the Temple of Apollo. Athletic and artistic competitions were also held, as they were in other parts of Greece.

Far right: A maritime nation naturally prizes its seafood. This market in Athens offers a great variety of fresh fish.

Right: Whatever the garment, you should find a button for it on this stall.

Below: A cheese stall in Chania, Crete's second city. Locally produced cheeses are readily available throughout Greece. The most common kind, crumbly and white, is *feta*, which is made from sheep's or goats' milk.

But what made Delphi special was the presence of the Oracle. Deep within the temple sat the Pythia, a woman who would chew laurel leaves and breathe fumes which seeped through a fissure in the rock until she fell into a trance. Then the temple priests would ask her to foretell the future on behalf of suppliants.

Not surprisingly under these circumstances, the voice of Apollo was often difficult to interpret. King Croesus of Lydia once asked if he should make war against the Persians. The oracle told him that if he did an empire would be lost. Croesus took this for a favorable omen, but in the event it was his own empire that was lost. But not every answer was ambiguous. When asked if there was anyone wiser than the philosopher Socrates, the answer was simply "No".

OSIAS LOUKAS AND DAPHNI

Today more than 95 per cent of Greeks belong to the Eastern Orthodox Church. Members of other religions are given complete freedom to practice, but everyone must be baptized and it is necessary to be registered with the Church in order to obtain an identity card or any kind of license. Black-robed priests are a familiar sight, and little wayside shrines dedicated to particular saints are to be found on every road in Greece.

The Greek Orthodox Church traces its history directly to the church founded by the disciples of Christ in Jerusalem after His death. The art and architecture of Greek churches and monasteries are usually in the Byzantine style, and among the greatest example of Byzantine culture in Greece are the monasteries of Osias Loukas and

Daphni — both within easy distance of Athens. Osias Loukas was named after a saint who lived in the tenth century. It possesses some very fine mosaics, especially a Nativity dating from the eleventh century, and wall paintings. The church, which is octagonal in shape, surmounted by a dome, was taken as a model by many later Greek church architects.

The monastery at Daphni, which also dates from the eleventh century, is renowned for its magnificent mosaic of Christ Pantokrator (meaning Almighty) in the central dome of the church. Fortified on the outside, the monastery offers an atmosphere of great tranquility within.

EPIDAURUS

Every spring pilgrims would make their

way to the small city state of Epidaurus. They came to celebrate the festival of Aesculapius, god of healing. There were strictly religious events, such as a formal procession from Epidaurus town to the sanctuary, bringing animals for sacrifice. Hymns were sung, and after the animals had been slaughtered it seems that everyone went off to the banqueting hall to eat them.

There were also athletic competitions, such as all-in wrestling, held in the stadium. And there were artistic contests in poetry, music and theater.

Unfortunately, almost all of the sanctuary was destroyed, first by earthquake and then quite possibly by the Emperor Constantine, who considered the cult of Aesculapius a threat to the new state

religion, Christianity. At any rate the temple, stadium, banqueting hall, hostels and other buildings, including a mysterious circular structure called the Thymele, have all been reduced to their foundations.

The theater survived, probably because as a result of the earthquake the auditorium was filled with earth. Excavations in the nineteenth century revealed the most beautiful and best-preserved theater from ancient times. Only the two-story stage building was gone. The auditorium held 16,000 spectators (rather more than the total population of Epidaurus town at that time), yet a whisper spoken on stage or from the circular orchestra can be clearly heard in the back row of seats without the need for artificial amplification.

Above: Tobacco leaves drying in the sun in Thrace, the northeastern province of Greece which borders on Bulgaria and Turkey.

Above left: The White Tower, viewed along the waterfront in Thessaloniki. This forbidding edifice, built by the Venetians in the fifteenth century, was once part of the city's maritime defenses. It is also known as the Bloody Tower: in 1826 a company of janissaries was massacred within its walls on the order of Sultan Mahmud II.

Below left: A goatherd tends his flock in the rolling hills of the Halkidiki Peninsula.

Far left: Perhaps the most beautiful building at Delphi is the Tholos. Built around 370 BC, it is a circular construction raised on three steps. It possessed a conical roof, and was elaborately decorated, but its function remains a mystery.

Left: A monastery on the sacred peninsula of Mount Athos. Monks have sought tranquility here for 1000 years, and the tradition of Byzantine monasticism remains alive.

Below: Very little of the land in Greece is flat. Some of the hilliest country has been reclaimed for cultivation through terracing.

The theater at Epidaurus was built some time in the fourth or third century BC. By this time Aesculapius had already made the transition from famous – but mortal – physician to god of healing. Although it is not complete, this is the best preserved of all Greek theaters. The beautiful symmetry of its design has been famous since ancient times.

Above: Although only the six rings of stone forming the foundations of the Thymele or Tholos at Epidaurus are still in place, archeologists have been able to reconstruct how the whole building must have looked. This lion head was one of many which adorned the rim of the roof.

Left: This mosaic of St. Paul, dating from the eleventh century, is to be found in the main church of Osias Loukas monastery. Practically every inch of wall space in this church is covered with mosaics, which took over 100 years to complete.

47

Above: A distant view of the acropolis of Mycenae in the Peloponnese. The Mycenaeans preferred their buildings to be strong rather than beautiful.

Right: This golden octopus brooch was found among a mass of treasures in the shaft graves at Mycenae, and testifies to the wealth and power of the city state.

Far right: Mycenae's famous Lion Gate, built around 1250 BC. Six hundred years later the architects of Athens marveled at the huge scale of these walls. They called them "Cyclopean" because they said that only the Cyclops, legendary one-eyed giants, could have raised such enormous stones.

Cool evening hours are the perfect time to sit in peace. This waterside church is in Aegina.

CHAPTER 5

Jewels of the Aegean

After the decline of the Minoans around 1500 BC, control over the Greek world fell into the hands of the Mycenaeans. They are named after their most important city state, though there were in fact several independent and not always mutually friendly centers in Mycenaean civilization.

The Mycenaeans were warriors and adventurers — the heroes of Homer's poems. They built massive fortresses rather like the baronial halls of medieval Europe. The city fortress of Mycenae boasts walls in places over 20 ft thick, and they were probably 30 ft high. Beneath the main gate can still be seen the ruts made by chariot wheels. Above it there is a lintel weighing 118 tons, and on top of that the famous lionesses, symbols of the power within. The structure is in fact so huge that it remains a mystery how it was ever erected.

Dug into the hillside beyond the gate, a 40-ft passageway leads to the Tomb of Agamemnon. This extraordinary beehive-shaped building is composed of 33 concentric rings of dry stone slabs, and the roof rises 43 ft at its center. Inside the fortress walls are the royal shaft graves where glorious objects of gold, silver and bronze were discovered in 1876. Mycenae was, it seems, as rich in gold as the legends proclaimed.

Much of this wealth, it must be said, was loot from one or another military expedition. The greatest of these adventures was the one described by Homer — the siege of Troy. Under the command of Agamemnon, King of Mycenae, a coalition of warriors from many states set sail in 1200 ships to rescue Helen — or that was their story: the true motive was probably to capture the Black Sea trade. Although they did defeat Troy in the end, the war marked the end of Mycenaean military domination.

Above: The harbor at Aegina. Here fishing vessels, sightseeing boats and private yachts tie up side by side. Larger ferries call frequently from Piraeus. In the evening the sidewalks are full to overflowing with the restaurants' clientele. Here you can also hire a horse-drawn carriage for trips around the island.

Far right: As in all great civilizations, the Greeks care not only about the function but also about the beauty of even everyday objects. Fishing nets, boats and balconies all make their contribution to the appreciation of life.

Legend tells that on his return from the war, Agamemnon was murdered in the bath by his wife, Clytemnestra. She herself was a slave, so she had motive enough. There is certainly evidence that the Mycenaeans suffered from civil wars as well as exhaustion from the Trojan expedition. They were no match for the invading Dorians, and their civilization was crushed. Mycenae itself lay buried, but not quite forgotten, for 3000 years.

AEGINA

Just 16 miles across the Saronic Gulf from Athens lies the island of Aegina. As the steamer, heading from Piraeus, passes the lighthouse of Salamis, Aegina comes into view. The Temple of Aphaia is visible high in the green-brown hills. Before long we are navigating the shallow channel leading into Aegina's oval harbor.

Greeks as well as tourists commonly make the trip to visit the Monastery of Aghios Nectarios, Orthodox Christianity's most recent saint who died in the 1920s, but the evening boat will most likely be carrying Athenians escaping the heat of the capital to dine in the restaurants which line the harborside.

In summer, sailing boats will throng the waters, jostling brightly painted caiques laden with fruit, vegetables and fish, for Aegina's life is centered on the sea. In ancient times this island was a great naval power, rival to Athens herself. Aegina was the first state in Europe to issue coinage (around the seventh century BC), and her credit was good throughout the civilized world. But she was too close to Athens for comfort, and besides she was allied with Athens' arch-enemy, Sparta. So it was inevitable that she should be destroyed. It happened during the fifth century BC, and the Athenians were nothing if not thorough.

They deported the whole population, first hacking off their thumbs so that they could never again wield spears.

Today it is difficult to imagine such a turbulent past as young men and women, dressed in their finest, promenade along the waterfront in early evening.

CORFU AND THE IONIAN ISLANDS

History as well as geography has set the Ionian Islands apart from mainland Greece. Corfu is bathed in a gentle, almost Western European atmosphere, for, while the rest of Greece fell under Turkish rule, the Venetian Republic held sway here from the fourteenth to eighteenth centuries. Many of the buildings which gave Corfu Town its civilized charm date from this period, while others were added by the empires of France and Britain.

The most surprising legacy of British occupation is the game of cricket, played every Saturday in summer on the

Above: An Orthodox patriarch, resplendent in his gold-embroidered robes, leads a religious procession on Aegina.

Esplanade Square. Spectators sit outside elegant cafés supping *tsintsi birra* — the local version of the very English ginger beer — as they admire the players' skill. But the bray of a donkey soon breaks the spell, for Corfu is Greek, and proud to be so.

Spring is glorious. Wild flowers of every shade cover the island beneath the silver-green of Corfu's olive groves. From Mount Pantokrator lush valleys unfold to south and west like creases in a tapestry, and beyond them spreads Homer's "wine-dark sea". To the east, and only three miles away, vast and empty hills roll toward the hinterland of mysterious Albania.

It is this unique combination of West and East, humid winter and sparkling summer, which accounts for Corfu's popularity with tourists today. Half a million visitors every year have left their scars on the face of a small island. But Corfu remains a charming and welcoming place, unique in culture and natural beauty.

SANTORINI

Once there stood on the island of Thira a city of 30,000 souls. A colony of the great Minoan civilization based in Crete, Thira grew rich and developed a glorious culture to rival Knossos itself. Then, around 1500 BC, earthquakes began to shake the island. Soon they became so violent that the population had to leave. A small group stayed behind — probably a task force charged with the job of salvaging whatever they could, or protecting the city in readiness for more settled times.

But some years after the evacuation there occurred the biggest volcanic eruption known to history. For comparison, when the island of Krakatoa was destroyed in a volcanic explosion in 1883, it created a shock wave 50 ft high and the explosion was heard 2000 miles away. The eruption on Thira was five times as big. Most of the island disappeared beneath the sea, leaving a depression 32 miles across and about 200

Left: Corfu Town or Kerkira as it is generally known locally, is often described as the most beautiful city in Greece. It is certainly the most elegant, combining elements of architecture from several West European civilizations. This narrow street is in the old part of the town.

Above: Street markets are to be found everywhere in Corfu Town. The island's mild climate ensures an excellent choice of fruits and vegetables.

fathoms deep. Not only Thira perished, but the parent civilization of Crete was shattered at the same time, and never recovered.

If this story sounds familiar, it is probably because in the fourth century before Christ the philosopher Plato retold an old Egyptian legend: "There occurred violent earthquakes and floods; and in a single day and night of misfortune… Atlantis… disappeared in the depths of the sea." So perished a city "pre-eminent in courage and military skill, the leader of the Hellenes".

The idea that Thira — or Santorini, as it is often known — is the lost Atlantis would be the merest fancy, except for the work of the archeologist Spiros Marinatos. Beginning in 1967 Professor Marinatos and his team uncovered beneath many feet of ash Akrotiri, a great city of two- and three-story buildings, magnificently preserved. The work of excavation continues, and with it unfolds one of the great mysteries of the past.

THE SPORADES

The Aegean Sea was always the hunting ground of pirates — rich pickings were to be had from east-west trade. What better place to hide out than Sporades? The seas look calm, but they can be treacherous. A small and well-protected harbor topped by a fortified town precariously balanced on a cliff edge — just the recipe for a corsair's lair.

Gone are the pirates, and their clifftop fortresses are now mostly ruined by earthquakes. So for many years the islands of Skiathos, Skopelos, Skyros and Alonnissos lay forgotten. No Classical ruins beckoned foreigners to their shores.

But if you are looking for a beautiful spot, follow the Greeks. Skiathos in particular is very popular among Athenians in search of a week away from it all. They know that Koukounares beach is the most beautiful in all Greece. The island has a mantle of pine trees which gives it a gentle charm quite unlike anything to be found elsewhere. And the town of Skiathos offers waterside tavernas where superb food can be supped by candlelight, or evening hours slip by to the clack of backgammon chips as fishermen clean their nets.

EASTERN AEGEAN

Along the eastern edge of the Aegean, sometimes within sight of the Turkish mainland, are a string of islands known as the Dodecanese. With the exception of Kos, which has recently become popular particularly with younger visitors, these islands are perhaps the least affected by the

Old olive trees fashioned by time into haunting shapes in this Paros grove. On other islands the olive trees are polled to ensure that they remain close to the ground. The fruits are generally caught in nets laid beneath the trees.

impact of tourism. For many Greeks, life continues much as it has done for centuries.

Every island is unique, and each has its special attractions. Calymnos is renowned for its sponges. Diving for sponges is a dangerous occupation, so it is only right that there should be a splendid religious ceremony to bless the divers' boats.

Patmos is famous as the place where St. John wrote the Revelations. A rocky island, it is dominated by a huge monastery which looks more like a castle than a religious building. Samos, in contrast, is a green and abundant land. Further north lies Chios, the island which claims to be the birthplace of the poet Homer. Its capital is an attractive little town, though now its beauty is somewhat faded.

Beyond Chios lies Lesbos, well known for its association with the poet Sappho. Rich in history, Lesbos is a very attractive island, green and fertile, boasting particularly good ouzo and wine.

RHODES
Rhodes is in every way a romantic island. To watch the deep-red sun setting behind the coast of Turkey, 12 miles across the marble sea, is an unforgettable experience. Julius Caesar used to take his vacations here, and in that, at any rate, he made a good choice.

Rhodes was inhabited as long ago as 2000 BC, and some evidence of Minoan settlement remains. But it was the Dorians who built the acropolis at Lindos, with its Temple of Athena which rivals even Athens in splendor. Lindos was in fact the island's capital. It boasted two harbors, which are now delightful beaches below a picturesque little town.

Rhodes Town itself was founded in 408 BC, and a vast undertaking it must have been, since there was no good natural harbor. Tradition has it that the 90-ft Colossus, a monument to Helios the Sun God, bestrode the present-day Mandraki Harbor. This Wonder of the World certainly existed — though not there. It remained upright for only 75 years before an earthquake toppled it, and lay on its side for 900 years, probably where the Palace of the Knights now stands, before Saracens carved it up and sold it for scrap in AD 635.

Right: Mules (above) are the recommended means of transportation on the volcanic island of Santorini. One look at the road between town and harbor (below) explains why. There are 587 steps.

Below: Lawrence Durrell has written of Santorini that "the reality is so astonishing that prose and poetry, however winged, will forever be forced to limp behind." The capital, Fira, teeters on the edge of a 900-foot drop into the deep blue waters of the bay below.

The Palace of the Grand Masters of the Ancient Order of the Knights of St. John of Jerusalem (to give this glorious building its proper title) stands atop a hill overlooking the town. The Knights ruled Rhodes for 200 years during the tempestuous era of the Crusades. They were of many nationalities, as a stroll down the Street of the Knights will show. Lining the narrow ways are the Inns of the Tongues, where Crusaders from Provence, Spain, France, Italy, Auvergne, England and Germany used to live.

Many and glorious were the exploits of the knights. Most famous was their last act: for half a year, in 1522, 600 of them withstood attack from 100,000 Saracens led by Suleiman the Magnificent, before finally being forced to surrender. In recognition of their valor, the conquerors gave them safe passage to Malta — remarkable chivalry for those days.

For the next 400 years Rhodes was ruled by the Turks, as the Mosque of Suleiman and other monuments attest. Italian and then German occupation followed, and it was only in 1948 that Rhodes was re-united with Greece.

Left: Rooftops on Skyros, largest of the Sporades Islands.

Below: The Greeks are renowned for their leatherwork. Bags, shoes and sandals spill out of shops and stalls wherever you go. It is common for a shoe vendor to offer potential customers a cup of coffee or a glass of *ouzo* – a gesture which is half traditional hospitality, and half shrewd sales technique!

CRETE

Crete was fashioned on a grand scale. About 120 miles in length, it is by far the largest island in the Aegean. A huge mountain range dominates the landscape wherever you go. The slopes are not green but purple with flowers of the oregano bush, filling the air with its glorious aroma as the sun bakes the earth.

There are delightful and picturesque spots, to be sure. Aghios Nikolaos, a village grown into a substantial holiday town around a harbor and lake, offers delightful tavernas on the water's edge. Chania's Venetian port and parts of the capital Heraklion speak of the civilized life. And at the eastern end of the island Vai springs a surprise—Europe's only palm forest, mantling a cluster of golden beaches.

But Crete has never been a safe and comfortable place, and it is not long before the elements reassert their dominance. A

howling, blistering wind from North Africa, called the *sirocco,* may catch the unwary. Twisted and turned by the labyrinthine valleys, it will appear from the east, reverse direction and vanish as abruptly as it came.

It was a natural catastrophe, or a series of catastrophes, that brought to an end the extraordinary civilization of the Minoans. Where these people came from is not known, but they settled in Crete around 2600 BC. They were considerably more advanced than the New Stone Age peoples whom they displaced: they worked copper and bronze, showed sophisticated craft in their treatment of pottery, and evidently conducted extensive trade from the earliest times.

Over the next 1000 years or so, the Minoans developed an empire based on trade throughout the Aegean and centered on the great palace at Knossos. Legend told of a fearful bull-like monster, the Minotaur, which inhabited a labyrinth here. The complexity of the township probably inspired the labyrinth idea. As for the Minotaur, it is known that the Minoans excelled in leaping over the backs of charging bulls. Minos himself was the Priest-King of Knossos, and doubtless an awesome figure.

Around 1600 BC Knossos and the other palace centers at Phaistos, Mallia and Zakros were severely damaged by an earthquake. They were restored, and then about 1450 BC they all seem to have been simultaneously destroyed. It is not yet possible to be certain, but the most likely explanation is that the vast volcanic explosion at Santorini produced an earthquake, tidal wave and deluge of volcanic ash which made Crete, or most of it, quite uninhabitable. The Minoan civilization was wiped out.

Over the centuries Crete fell under the control of a succession of rulers, Mycenaean, Dorian, Roman, Byzantine, Arab, Venetian and Turkish. During the nineteenth century, in common with the rest of Greece, the Cretans took up arms to fight for their independence. The new Greek state was proclaimed in 1832, but for Crete the struggle was not over. Every decade there were uprisings to the rallying cry of "Freedom or Death!" The island was granted its own independence in 1898, and was formally united with the rest of Greece in 1913.

The fighting was not over, however, for Crete was subjected to a particularly brutal occupation and guerrilla war against the Germans after 1941. Entire villages were ruined and their inhabitants shot in reprisal for the continuing resistance.

Harsh memories linger from those days up in the mountains, but nothing has altered the traditional warmth and hospitality offered to visitors. The people of Crete are tough, proud and generous — qualities forged by their history and terrain.

Right: Kithira, an island midway between the mainland and Crete, claims to be the birthplace of Aphrodite, goddess of love. A romantic island it certainly is, though some explain the legend by pointing to the rocky shores and reminding us that the Greek word *aphros* means "foam".

Far right: Light and color, the elements which endow Greece with its unique and spellbinding atmosphere. The picture above was taken in the village of Lindos on Rhodes; the stairway below is on Calymnos in the Dodecanese group.

Above: This whitewashed church is on the island of Patmos, most northerly of the Dodecanese. It was on Patmos that St. John wrote the *Apocalypse* – but these children are in more lighthearted mood!

Left: A coffee house on Chios. The remarkable ornamentation is typical of Chios, which owes much of its charm to the impression of faded opulence.

Far left: Samos has always been a prosperous and abundant island. This church interior in Vathi, the capital, has been built on a grand scale uncommon on the Aegean islands.

Far right: A sponge fisherman washes his day's crop before taking it up into town to market.

Right: Donkeys and mules still play a central role in the life of the Greek peasant. This family is seen, goats and all, traveling a dusty road in the mountains of Crete.

Below: Plowing fields in Crete. The method has not changed for centuries. The hillside in the background is covered in oregano, which gives the air a delicious scent.

Above: In Rhodes it is still possible to find carpets which have been woven by hand. The technique is just the same as that used in Iran, where the more famous Persian rugs are made.

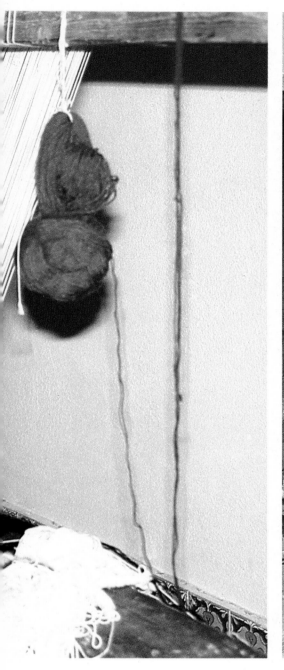

Left: The Greeks are passionately involved with family life. In the countryside it is still common for a bride to bring her husband a dowry. In general, women's position in Greek society is more traditionally subservient than would be acceptable elsewhere in the West. This group is from Rhodes.

Above: The Government Building in Rhodes Town. Gothic and Islamic influences have been subtly blended in this elegant modern structure.

Things to see in Greece and the Greek Islands

Athens: Acropolis

BULGARIA

ALBANIA

MACEDONIA

Thessaloniki

THRACE

Corfu

EPIROS

⑩

⑧

THESSALY

Northern
Sporades

Lesbos

AEGEAN SEA

TURKEY

IONIAN ISLANDS

STEREA

④

EVVOIA

ELLAS

⑨ ① ②
③ Athens/Piraeus
⑥
Aegina
⑤ ⑪

PELOPONNESE

CYCLADES

DODECANESE
(SPORADES)

⑫

⑭

⑬ RHODES

CRETE

Iraklion

⑯ ⑮

Delphi

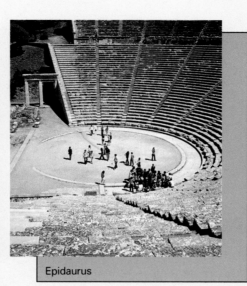

Epidaurus

Santorini

Mycenae

1 Athens: Acropolis
Site of the Parthenon and other major monuments from the Golden Age of Greek civilization. Not to be be missed is the Acropolis Museum, which houses most of the Parthenon frieze and many statues which originally stood in the temples of the Acropolis itself.

2 Athens: National Archeological Museum
Deservedly recognized as one of the world's greatest museums. Here treasures are on display which have been collected from every important center of ancient Greek civilization.

3 Athens: Plaka
Tumbledown quarter of the old city, clinging to the northeast slope of the Acropolis. Narrow streets are packed with *tavernas* and market stalls. Focus of Athens nightlife.

4 Delphi
Ancient center of the cult of Apollo and seat of the Pythian Oracle. Magnificent ruins stand on the slopes of Mount Parnassus, commanding breathtaking views. Drink from the river Lethe, the Waters of Forgetfulness, and leave your cares behind!

5 Mycenae
Fortress capital of the powerful civilization whose most famous king was Agamemnon. Here are the Lion Gate, the beehive tombs, and the royal shaft graves.

6 Epidaurus
Ancient religious center dedicated to Aesculapius, god of healing. Greece's most magnificent theater is to be found here.

7 Mount Athos
This autonomous religious community, sited on a peninsula in the northeast, traces its history back 1000 years. Twenty monasteries, some possessing magnificent artistic treasures, are still occupied. Women are not permitted on Mount Athos.

8 Meteora
Monasteries were built hundreds of feet in the sky, atop sheer cliffs, by monks seeking seclusion and detachment from the world. Some may now be visited – by those who have a head for heights!

9 Corinth
Here the Roman Emperor Nero dug the first traces of a canal with a golden spade – but the rock was too tough for the engineers of those times. The canal was in fact completed in 1893 with the aid of British dynamite. It was 6939 yards long, but only 75 feet wide. Small ferries make the dramatic passage.

10 Olympia
In this sanctuary, dedicated to Zeus, the ancient Greeks laid down their weapons once every four years and joined in peaceful competition in the Olympic Games. This tradition lasted for ten centuries from 776 BC. Many impressive ruins remain, including the Temple of Hera and the Stadium itself. The starting blocks for running events are still in place.

11 Cape Sounion
Here, some 35 miles south of Athens, stands the elegant fifth-century BC Temple of Poseidon, looking from a rocky headland across the Saronic Gulf. Unforgettable at sunset. Lord Byron scratched his name on a column of this temple!

12 Santorini
Mysterious volcanic island rising spectacularly out of the Southern Aegean. Once center of a great Minoan civilization, suddenly destroyed by natural disaster, Santorini is famous for the giddy clifftop location of its main town Fira, and for its black beaches.

13 Rhodes: Lindos
Here are combined the attractions of a magnificent ancient acropolis, including the Temple of Athena, a picturesque whitewashed town and two sandy beaches.

14 Rhodes Town
Many fascinating medieval buildings remind the visitor of Rhodes' romantic past as a headquarters of the Crusaders. The Saracens, too, left impressive monuments to their occupation of the island.

15 Crete: Knossos
A few miles from Heraklion stands the capital of the Minoan empire, 5000 years old. Much of the old town center remains, together with remarkable reconstruction done under the direction of British archeologist Sir Arthur Evans. The frescoes are not to be missed.

16 Crete: Gorge of Samaria
Not an excursion for the unfit, this. The Gorge of Samaria, ten miles from top to bottom, is the longest ravine in Europe. The journey, on foot, takes some eight hours and is not possible in the winter months. But the unrivaled beauty of the wild landscape easily justifies the exertion for the adventurous.

PICTURE CREDITS